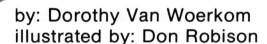

When All the World Was Waiting

An Advent Book for Children

by: Dorothy Van Woerkom
illustrated by: Don Robison
designed by: John D. Firestone & Associates, Inc.

CONCORDIA

Publishing House
St. Louis

To Norma Jean Durrett,
a very special librarian

Library of Congress Cataloging in Publication Data

Van Woerkom, Dorothy.
 When all the world was waiting.

 SUMMARY: Biblical quotations, stories, and suggested activities
explain the significance of Advent.
 1. Advent--Prayer-books and devotions--Juvenile literature.
[1. Advent--Prayer books and devotions.
 2. Prayer books and devotions] I. Title
BV40.V36   242′.33   79-9965
ISBN 0-570-03474-4

Concordia Publishing House, St. Louis, Missouri

PREFACE

When God made the world, it was a perfect place. There was no sadness or sickness or death. God gave the people He had created everything they needed to be happy.

But one day Satan, the devil, told them they could be even happier. They could be as wise as God if they would just eat the fruit from the tree that God had told them not to touch.

The people listened to Satan and ate the fruit. And God became very angry. To punish them for their disobedience, God, in his fatherly way, permitted many sorrows and troubles in their lives. Satan's power in the world grew stronger than ever, after the first sin had been committed.

But God still loved the people, and He was sorry for them. He promised to send them a Savior--a Messiah--who would come and destroy Satan's power over them.

Many years passed, and the Messiah did not appear. The people often became discouraged, but God would not let them forget His promise.

At last, when all the world was waiting, the Savior came. His name was Jesus, and He was born on Christmas Day in the city of Bethlehem. He was the Son of God.

Day 1

And I will put an enemy between you and this woman.
Genesis 3:15, The Holy Bible for Children

Adam and Eve lived in the Garden of Eden in the perfect world God had created for them. But God wanted to test their love for Him. He told them not to eat the fruit of a certain tree.

One day Satan appeared in the form of a snake. He wanted Adam and Eve to disobey God. He told Eve that the fruit from this tree would make her as wise as God. Eve believed Satan. She ate the fruit and she gave some to Adam. Together they committed the first sin ever committed.

God punished Adam and Eve for their disobedience. He drove them from the Garden forever. He sent sorrow and trouble for the rest of their lives. But, he never stopped loving them.

God looked down at Satan in anger. He said: The day will come when I will send Someone into the world to destroy your evil power over My people! This woman will have many children, and they will have many children. Some day, One of these will be your most dreaded enemy.

Activity:

Waiting is easier if we keep busy. Why not start the long Christmas wait by making an **Advent calendar.** Start by cutting 26 sheets of paper all the same size. Attach them together with a staple, paper clip, or string. Number the pages 1 through 26. Place 26 on top and number 1 on the bottom. Hang the calendar near your bed. Each morning when you wake, remove the top page. The number showing tells you how many days you have to wait before you celebrate the birth of Jesus.

Prayer:

Dear Lord, today begins the wait for the coming of the Lord Jesus Christ, my Savior. I will wait with love in my heart. Amen.

The man called his wife's name Eve, because she was the mother of all living.

Genesis 3:20, Revised Standard Version

(The name Eve in Hebrew resembles the word for living.)

Eve heard God's promise. She was filled with gladness and hope. Every time a child was born into the world, she wondered, "Is this the One? Is this the Child who will save us from the devil's power?"

But in Eve's long life, the Savior never came.

Activity:

While you are waiting, start making things for your family's celebration, by making **gift tags.** From old Christmas cards, cut out small gift tags in different shapes. If you have a pair of pinking shears you can cut fancy edges.

Prayer:

Lord God, You know all things and have promised me salvation and life with You in heaven. Give me a heart that trusts You fully. Send Your Holy Spirit to give me a strong faith when I read and hear Your promises. Take away all doubt and fear. Show me that You are the almighty God, who keeps His promises. Help me to believe with all my heart. Amen.
(From Dear Father in Heaven, © 1963, 1977, Concordia Publishing House)

Now the earth was corrupt in God's sight, and the earth was filled with violence. And God saw the earth, and behold, it was corrupt; for all flesh had corrupted their way upon the earth.
Genesis 6:11-12, Revised Standard Version

Adam and Eve had many children. Their children had children, and their children's children had children. Now many people lived on the earth, and these were called descendants of Adam and Eve.

Soon Satan was busy telling them all to forget about God and to pray to false gods. The people obeyed Satan, and forgot about God's promise.

Activity:

During your wait for Jesus to come, make **bookmarks** for your friends and relatives. Use any material you wish: colored paper, felt, or pieces of material. Cut strips 2 inches wide and 6 inches long. Decorate them any way you choose.

Prayer:

Dear Father in Heaven,
Help me to be more patient.
Help me to be more at peace with myself.
Help me to be more considerate of others.
Help me to love others, as I know you love us.
Amen.

15 16 17 18 19 20 21 22 23 24 25 26

And no longer will your name be Abram. [From now on] your name shall be Abraham, because I have made you the father of many nations.

Genesis 17:5, The Holy Bible for Children

But there was one man who still believed in the one true God. His name was Abram. Abram was an old man. His wife, Sarai, was an old woman.

Abram owned flocks of sheep and herds of cattle and many servants. He was a rich man--except for one thing. He and Sarai had no children.

One day God said to Abram, "Leave your home and go to a land where I will lead you. I will bless you, and I will make your name a great name. You will be the father of many nations of people, and because of you I will bless all the families of the earth."

Then God changed Abram's name to Abraham which means "the father of many."

Activity:

Abraham believed in God, and he obeyed his command. Trace the journey of Abraham and his family to the new land.

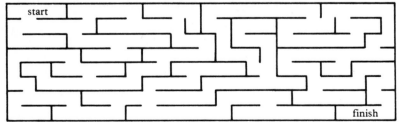

start

finish

Prayer:

O God, I know that I have not always obeyed my father and mother, my teachers and all whom You have placed over me. I confess that wanting my own ways gets me into trouble. Forgive these sins, I pray, and give me power to follow Your way even when it seems hard. Amen.

(From Dear Father in Heaven © 1963, 1977 Concordia Publishing House)

Through you all the families of the earth will be blessed.

Genesis 12:3, The Holy Bible for Children

God wanted Abraham to be the father of us all. He wanted our families, and all the families of the world, to be blessed in a special way because of His love for Abraham.

God gave this blessing to Abraham for a very special reason. He was reminding Abraham of the Promise He had given Eve. He was telling Abraham that the Savior, the Messiah, would one day be born into the family of Abraham's descendants.

Activity:

Make your own **Christmas Cards.** Fold a regular sheet of typing paper in half; fold it again. Decorate it with cut-outs from old Christmas cards, or decorate them with your own artwork. On the inside write your message. After you have made your Christmas Card list, make as many cards as you need.

Prayer:

Heavenly Father, hear my thanks
for Your loving care;
Help me now to show my love,
and each blessing share. Amen.
(From Dear Father in Heaven, © 1963,
1977 Concordia Publishing House)

I will multiply your descendants as the stars of the heaven, and . . . by your descendants all the nations of the earth shall bless themselves.
Genesis 26:4, Revised Standard Version

Abraham was a very old man when his son Issac was born. Isaac was not the Messiah, but he was the one God chose to receive the Promise. The Messiah would come into Isaac's branch of Abraham's great family. For this reason God gave Isaac a very special blessing.

"By your children and by your children's children, all the nations of the world shall be blessed," God told Isaac. "You will have as many descendants as there are stars in the sky."

Activity:

You still have a while to wait. Why not make a **Christmas Mobile** to hang in your room. Find a regular wire coat hanger. Cover it with colored strips of paper by wrapping it around the wire. Next cut Christmas shapes out of cardboard (the Star of Bethlehem, an angel, a candle, and many more). Tie yarn or string to one end of the shape, and then attach it to the coat hanger. Hang them at different lengths and in different positions.

Prayer:

Dear Father in heaven, I am fortunate to have loving parents, clothes to wear, a bed to sleep in, and food to eat. Bless someone tonight who is less fortunate than I. Amen.

I am God almighty: be fruitful and multiply; a nation and a company shall come from you, and kings shall spring from you.

Genesis 35:11, Revised Standard Version

Isaac married Rebecca. For many years they had no children, but Isaac never doubted God's promise that he would have as many descendants as there are stars in the sky.

When Isaac and Rebecca were both old, God blessed them with twin sons, Esau and Jacob. God chose Jacob to receive the Promise and the blessing.

"I am with you and I will protect you always," God told Jacob. God also changed Jacob's name to Israel.

Activity:

Do you know what an ancestor is? Do you know who your ancestors are? A fun project to do while you are waiting is to make a **Family Tree**. Start with yourself. List your brothers and sisters, then your mother and father, then their mother and father (your grandparents), and their parents, and their parents. Go back as far as you can. Ask your parents for help in putting your family tree together.

Prayer:

Dear Father in Heaven, Help my parents to live a life that is pleasing to You, that they may lead me to love You more and more. Amen.

Day 8

The land which I gave to Abraham and Isaac I will give to you, and I will give the land to your descendants after you.

Genesis 35:12, Revised Standard Version

Jacob had many sons, called the Sons of Israel. None of them was the Messiah, the Promised One. The people were becoming impatient. They were tired of waiting.

"Where is the Promised One?" they wondered. "When will He come?"

Activity:

God's people were impatient. They were getting tired of waiting. Try not to be impatient while you wait. Make **a puzzle**. Cut a large Christmas scene from a magazine. Paste it to a piece of cardboard. Cut the picture into twelve different pieces. Have fun with a friend or your family putting the puzzle together again.

Prayer:

Dear Lord, help me to love You in everything I do-- great or small. Help me to serve You and worship You in my heart, my mind, and in my deeds. Amen.

Day 1 2 3 4 5 6 7 8 9 10 11 12 13 14

I see Him, but not now; I behold Him, but not nigh: a Star shall come forth out of Jacob.

Numbers 24:17, Revised Standard Version

God heard the people. One day He sent a man named Balaam with a message.

"A great ruler will come from the family of Jacob," Balaam said. "One day I shall see Him, but not now. He is not yet near."

The people sighed. The knew the waiting was not over yet.

"Oh, send us the Messiah in our lifetime!" they prayed. But still the Messiah did not come.

Activity:

Remember that others are waiting with you. **Write a letter to a special friend** who lives far away, or maybe right around the corner. Let them know that you are thinking about them while you are waiting for the coming of our Lord Jesus.

Prayer:

Heavenly Father,
I am thankful for my friends, but You are my dearest Friend. Let me love all my friends as I know You love me. Amen.

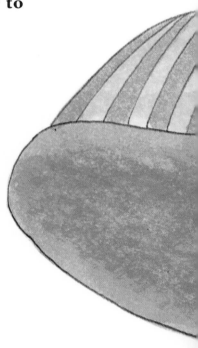

He chose the tribe of Judah.

Psalm 78:68, Revised Standard Version

Jacob had twelve sons. They were the grandsons of Isaac and the great-grandsons of Abraham. They were descendants of the large family God had promised Abraham and Isaac.

God wanted the Messiah to be born into the family of one of Jacob's sons. He chose Judah.

Activity:

Judah had 11 brothers. If you have a brother or a sister, think about them today, or a cousin or very good friend. Make them a **Christmas mobile** like you made for yourself earlier and give it to them to hang in their room.

Prayer:

God of all, help me to love my brothers and sisters. Help me to be patient with them and to understand that we are a family. Help us to be kind to one another, forgiving and honest. Bless them and keep them safe from all harm. Amen.

The scepter shall not depart from Judah ...until He comes to whom it belongs.

Genesis 49:10, Revised Standard Version

Jacob and his sons came to live in the land of Egypt. God allowed him to live many, many years. God let Jacob know that one of his twelve sons, Judah, would be the one to receive the promise.

At last it was time for Jacob to die. He called his sons around his bed. He gave each one a blessing, but to Judah he said, "Your branch of the family will lead all the others until the One we wait for comes to us at last."

Activity:

The time is getting nearer. The long wait is almost over. Ask your parents if you can **decorate your bedroom window.** Use regular white typing paper. Cut out Joseph, Mary, and the Baby Jesus in the Manger. Tape them to your window.

Prayer:

Dear Father, Your Son Jesus is coming, and it makes me so happy. It is a time to be joyful and glad. My prayer is that everyone will find the joy and happiness I feel today! Amen.

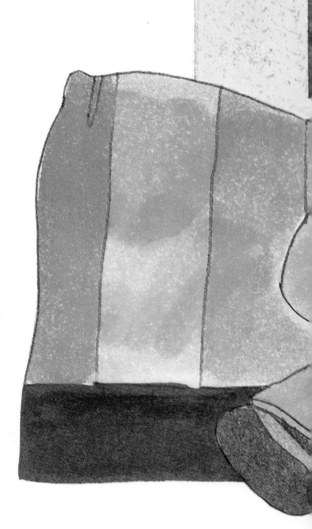

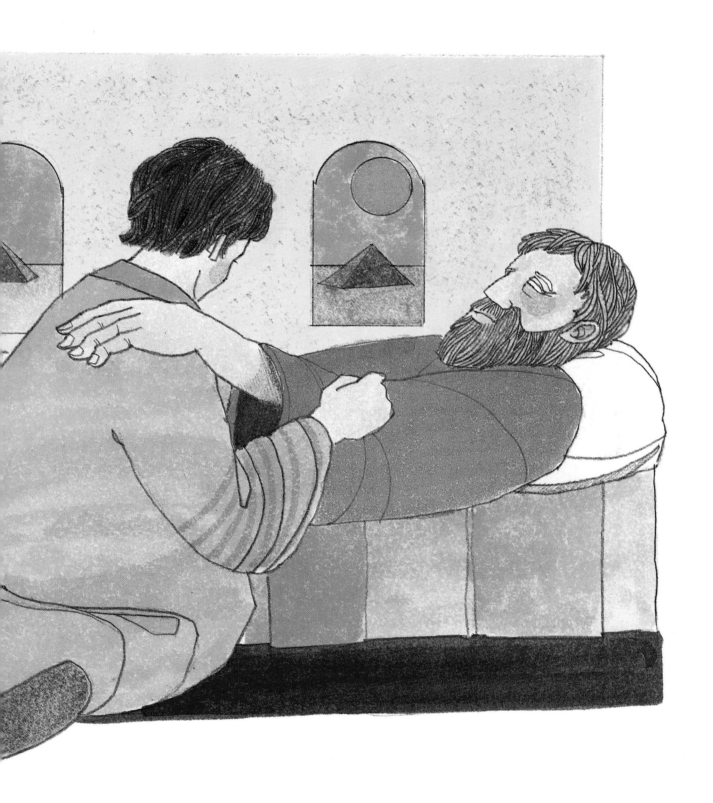

Someday a shoot will come out of the stump of Jesse, a new Branch will grow out of his roots.
Isaiah 11:1, The Holy Bible for Children

Many things happened to Jacob's descendants after he died. They suffered many hardships, but many remembered the promise God had made to Abraham, Isaac, Jacob, and Judah.

Judah became the chief of a large tribe of people with many families. From this tribe, God chose the family of Jesse. The Messiah would be born to one of Jesse's descendants.

Activity:

Even though it is winter and all the flowers are dead, you can still have flowers in your house. Maybe your parents have some seeds left from last year, or maybe you can find a store that has flower seeds. Fill some paper cups with dirt. Place two seeds in each cup. Place your cups in a sunny window and water them every three days. Watch what happens. You can give the cups to family and friends as gifts. Wrap the cups with foil and tie a colorful bow around each one.

Prayer:

God, thank You for all the beautiful things around me. Help me to see the world You made with eyes of gratitude. Help me to sing Your praises in all seasons and to appreciate the wisdom of Your deeds. Amen.

In that day the root of Jesse will be a hope for people. People of all nations will rally to Him because life with Him will be glorious.
Isaiah 11:10, The Holy Bible for Children

No one knew that the Messiah would come from the family of Jesse until God told His plan to the holy prophet, Isaiah, who told it to the people.

"The family of Jesse is like a great tree," Isaiah said. "The tree will have many branches, and from one of these branches the Messiah will come."

Activity:

Whether you live in the country or in the city, there are birds that are hungry. It is difficult for them to find food during the winter months. Pop some popcorn with your parent's help. Enjoy eating it with your family or friends. Save some. Place the remaining popcorn in a shallow pan and set it on the porch. The birds will come to eat, and you'll have an added treat watching them.

Prayer:

God, You are the creator of all things great and small. Help me to use this time to see Your goodness in the tiny creatures, flowers, animals, and birds. Fill my heart with love for You and Your great creation. Amen.

And the spirit of the Lord will be in Him, the spirit of wisdom, understanding, advice and power, the spirit of knowledge and the fear of the Lord.
Isaiah 11:2, The Holy Bible for Children

When the people heard Isaiah speak, they knew that it would be a long time yet before the Messiah would come.

Adam and Eve were dead. Abraham, Isaac, Jacob and Judah, and all the people who had lived in their times were dead. More people were born and lived and died, and still the waiting went on.

Soon Jesse would die, and many who lived in his days. The Messiah would not come in their lifetime.

Activity:

While you wait, play a game with your parents, brothers, or sisters, or you can play quietly by yourself. Start with the letter **A**. --How many names from the Bible can you name that begin with that? Then move to the letter **B**, then **C** and on through the alphabet. Add up the names at the end to see who has remembered the most.

Prayer:

Bless me as I study to learn more about You and Your wonderful deeds. Keep me strong in faith; guide me in my work and play. As your child, I put my trust in You. Be with me and those I love. Amen.

I will raise up for David a righteous Branch, and He shall reign as King and deal wisely.

Jeremiah 23:5, Revised Standard Version

David was the son of Jesse. He was the greatest of the Hebrew kings from the tribe of Judah. God loved David and chose him to receive the Promise.

David was the grandson of Judah, who was the grandson of Isaac, who was the son of Abraham. God wanted the Messiah to come from David's branch of Abraham's great family.

Activity:

Make a **crossword puzzle.** Name those to whom God promised the Messiah: Isaac, Abraham, David, Eve, Jesse, Jacob, Judah.

Prayer:

Dear Father in Heaven, Open my eyes so that I may clearly see and understand Your blessings. Love is needed everywhere, but as I want to be loved, I must also love others. Amen.

I will make your name great. When you die, your son will build a house for My name . . . and your throne will be established forever.
2 Samuel 7:12, 13, The Holy Bible for Children

Of the increase of his government . . . there shall be no end, upon the throne of David.
Isaiah 9:7, Revised Standard Version

When God was ready to tell David His plan, He called upon a holy man named Nathan.

"Go and tell David what I say," God told Nathan. "Tell him that the Messiah will be born to someone in David's family. I will be His Father, and He will be My Son, and He will rule the world forever."

Nathan hurried to do as God commanded. When Nathan had finished speaking to David, David prayed to God.

"Who am I, Lord, that you have given me this Promise? But You have said it, and all my family will be blessed forever."

Activity:

Make an **Advent wreath** with the help of your parents or sisters and brothers. There are many ways to make the wreath.

Prayer:

Dear God, help me to understand, like King David, that You have a plan for my life. Let me believe that everything fits together and works for my good. Open my heart to know Your will that I may love and trust You all the days of my life. Amen.

The Lord swore to David a sure oath from which He will not turn back: "One of the sons of your body I will set on your throne."
Psalm 132:11, Revised Standard Version

David lived for many years and died believing God's Promise. For many long years after he had died, the people waited.

"When will the Promised One come?" they asked each other. "And when He comes, how will we know Him? The family of David is now large and scattered."

Activity:

Do you know what a tradition is? A tradition is something you do every year at the same time. Why don't you **help start a tradition in your family.** Something you do together as a family every year during Advent. Talk it over with your parents, and decide together what your tradition will be, and on what day.

Prayer:

Dear Father in Heaven, I want to keep on growing in Your loving care. Help me to be patient and understanding, and when I am tempted to sin, give me the strength to resist. I trust You are with me and will never leave me, because I am Your child. Amen.

Therefore the Lord Himself will give you a sign; behold, a virgin shall conceive and bear a Son and shall call His name Immanuel.

Isaiah 7:14, King James' Version

The people begged for a sign and God heard them. He sent the holy prophet Isaiah to tell them what this sign would be.

"Here is the sign which the Lord will give you," Isaiah said. "A young woman will have a son. She will call Him by a name which means 'God with us.' By His name you will know He is the One."

Activity:

Can you finish this message from Isaiah 9:6?

F _ r   t _   _ s   _   c h _ l d   _ s

b _ r n ,   _ n t _   _ s   _   s _ n   _ s

g _ v _ n .

Prayer:

Dear heavenly Father, as Christmas draws near, help me to remember that Christmas is Your very own Son's birthday. As I get ready to celebrate the day at home and at church, remind me that Christmas is not just one day but every day I live, if Your dear Son is in my heart. Amen.

"Behold the days are coming," says the Lord, "when I will raise up for David a righteous Branch, and he shall reign as king and deal wisely, and shall execute justice and righteousness in the land."

Jeremiah 23:5, Revised Standard Version

In those days God spoke to many men who prophesied the coming of the Messiah. The people listened to them. They wanted to hear more! Isaiah, one of the prophets of God, began to tell them how God said it would be when the Messiah finally came into the world.

"Those who walked in darkness will see a great light," he said. "For to us a child is born; to us a Son is given! He will rule all the world, and His name shall be called Wonderful, Counselor, Mighty God, Everlasting Father, Prince of Peace."

Activity:

Make Christmas tree decorations while you wait. String popcorn, or make a paper chain out of colored paper.

Prayer:

God, today I have tried to be kind and loving to those around me. Forgive me if I did not always succeed and grant me the strength to grow in Your saving grace. Amen.

O Bethlehem, you are little among the many towns in Judah. But from out of you I will bring someone who is to be ruler of Israel. Micah 5:2, The Holy Bible for Children

And nations shall come to Your light, and kings to the brightness of Your rising. Isaiah 60:3, Revised Standard Version

The ox knows its owner, and the ass its master's crib. Isaiah 1:3, Revised Standard Version

Another holy man spoke about another sign. This man's name was Micah. "The Promised One will be born in Bethlehem, the city of David," Micah said.

"Kings will come from far places to see Him," Isaiah said. "They will come bringing precious gifts, and they will praise Him. Even the poorest of beasts, the ox and the donkey, will know Him when He comes."

The people listened and waited.

Activity:

Draw a picture of the little town of Bethlehem. What do you think it looked like when they were waiting for the Messiah to come? Hang your picture in your room, and think about the people who lived there: the innkeeper, the shepherds, the rich, the poor, the travelers. They had been waiting so long. Little did they know the long wait was almost over.

Prayer:

Dear Lord, thank You for this day. Thank You for watching me all the day through. Keep me through the night, and wake me with the morning light. Amen.

Day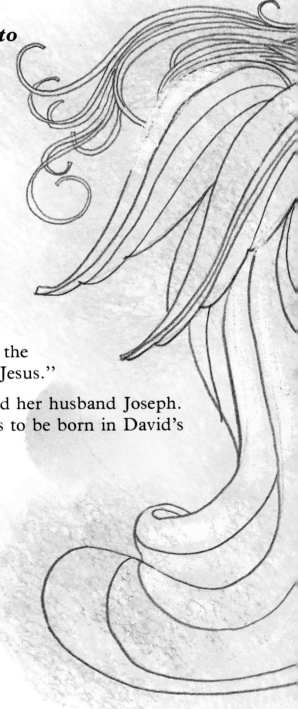

So all the generations from Abraham to David were fourteen generations, and from David to the deportation to Babylon fourteen generations, and from the deportation to Babylon to the Christ fourteen generations.
Matthew 1:17, Revised Standard Version

And so for 4,000 years the people had waited. They had been born, and lived, and died, and more had come to take their place on earth. Now these were waiting.

At last God was ready. He sent His angel to Mary, a young woman of Nazareth.

"You are to be the mother of God's own Son!" the angel told Mary. "And you shall call His name Jesus."

Mary belonged to the family of David, and so did her husband Joseph. But they lived in Nazareth--and the Messiah was to be born in David's city of Bethlehem!

Activity:

Make a soap carving of the Lord's angel. Use a regular bar of soft soap. Draw the outline of an angel on the front. Carefully using a kitchen knife cut out the shape. You can also use a candle.

Prayer:

Dear Lord, look down upon our home with love. We are ever thankful for Your gifts that are full and free. Amen.

In those days the Roman ruler Augustus sent out a royal command. All the people in his empire were to register for taxing.
Luke 2:1, The Holy Bible for Children

God had a plan to bring Mary and Joseph to Bethlehem. There was a new law which said that everyone who belonged to the family of David must go to Bethlehem to be counted and taxed. God knew that Mary and Joseph would obey this law and leave Nazareth at once.

Activity:

Bring Mary and Joseph from Nazareth to Bethlehem.

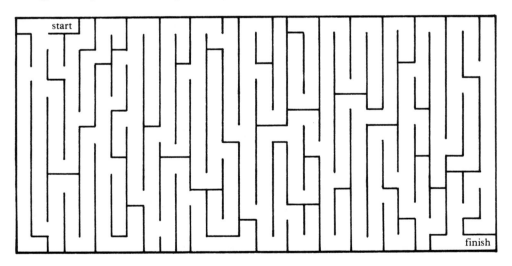

start

finish

Prayer:

Dear Lord, my heart is full of gladness. Open my heart so that I might be ready for the great gift You sent us--the Lord Jesus Christ, our Lord and Savior. Amen.

15 16 17 18 19 20 21 23 24 25 26

22

...and the leopard and goat will lie down together. Calves and fat cattle will be safe among lions, and a little child will lead them.

Isaiah 11:6, The Holy Bible for Children

When Mary and Joseph reached Bethlehem, the city was so crowded that there was no place for them to stay. They had to move into a cave where an ox was sheltered. They brought their own little donkey into the cave and put him near the ox.

Activity:

Draw the Nativity scene. Think about Mary and Joseph and what it must have been like for them. Talk about your picture with your parents. Talk about how Mary and Joseph must have felt knowing that God's Son was going to be born very soon.

How do you feel?

Prayer:

Lord, You put the lights in the sky. As You watch over the stars, I know You watch over me. I thank You for being so good to me. Keep me safe. Amen.

Day 1 2 3 4 5 6 7 8 9 10 11 12 13 14

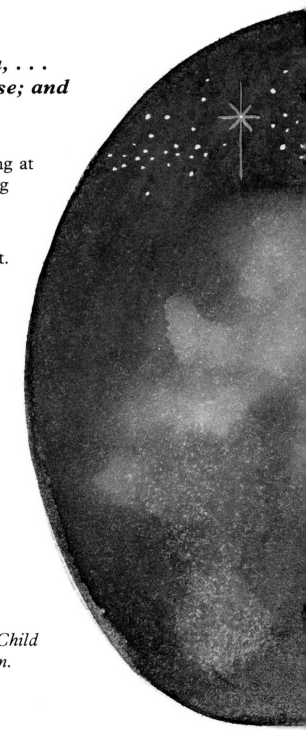

A multitude of camels shall cover you, . . .
They shall bring gold and frankincense; and
shall proclaim the praise of the Lord.
Isaiah 60:6, Revised Standard Version

Far away in another land some kings were looking at the sky. They saw the Star of Bethlehem moving across the heavens. They remembered that the people had been waiting for a Messiah.

"This must be the sign of His coming!" they thought.

So the kings gathered up their precious gifts of gold and frankincense and myrrh. They called their servants and their camels together and set out to follow the Star, just like the prophet Isaiah said God told him it would happen.

Activity:

Make a banner of paper or cloth. Trace a Christmas message on colored paper or cloth. Cut out the letters and glue them onto the banner. (Suggestions: JOY TO THE WORLD; OH, COME, ALL YE FAITHFUL; HARK! THE HERALD ANGELS SING.)

Prayer:

Dear Lord, it is so good to know that Jesus was a Child like me once. How much You must have loved Him. Thank You for sending Him to us. Amen.

15 16 17 18 19 20 21 22 23 25 26

24

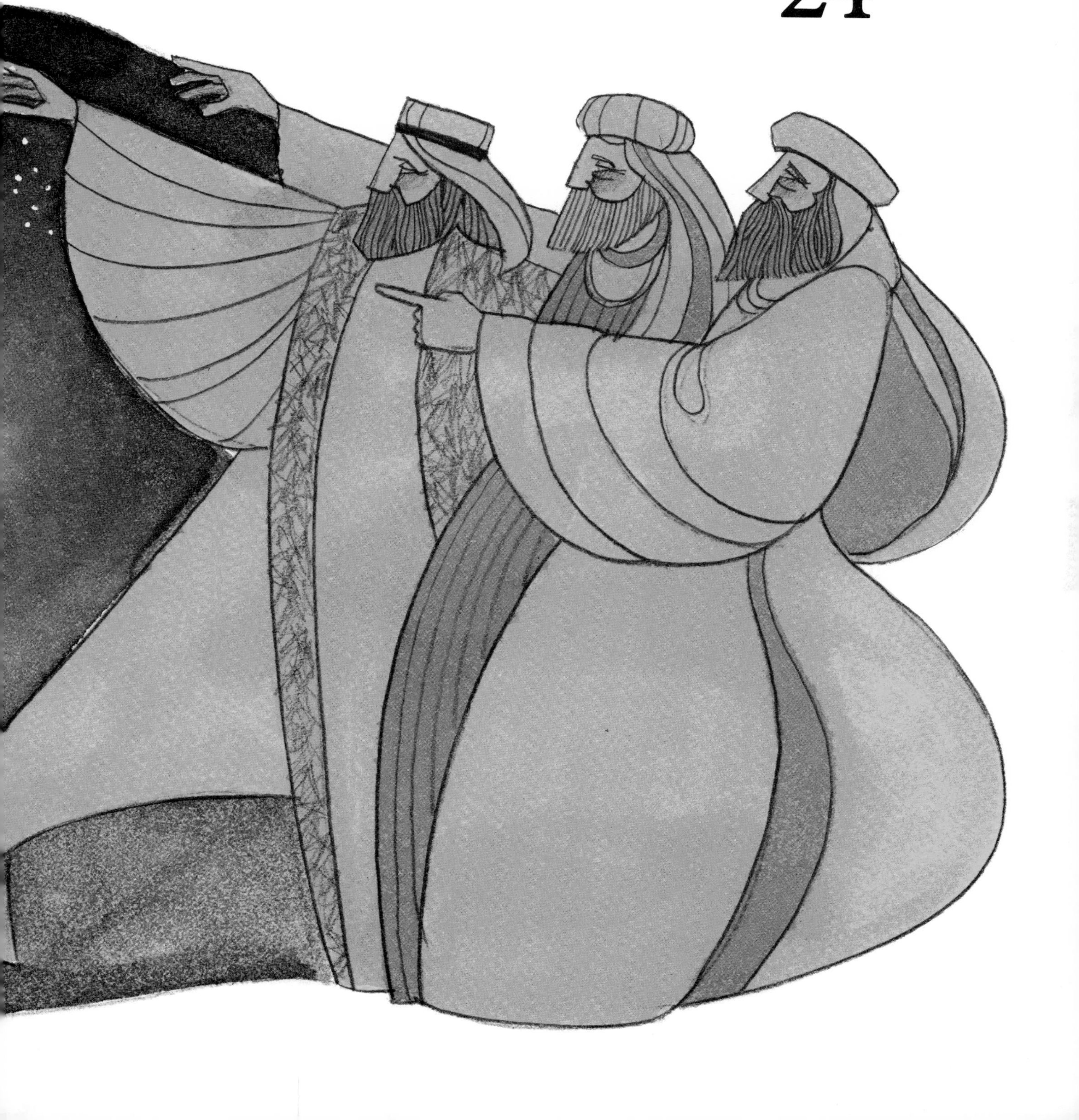

Day 1 2 3 4 5 6 7 8 9 10 11 12 13 14

And to Him was given dominion and glory and kingdom, that all people, nations, and languages should serve Him; His dominion is an everlasting dominion, which shall not pass away, and His kingdom one that shall not be destroyed.
Daniel 7:14, Revised Standard Version

In a lowly manger, wrapped in swaddling clothing, Jesus the Son of God was born.

And so it happened that of all the world's creatures, the ox and the donkey were the first, besides Mary and Joseph, to see the Holy Infant.

Activity:

God gave us the gift of Himself. This was a very special gift. Then He gave us the gift of each other. Think of something you can make or do as a very special gift for someone you love.

Prayer:

Dear Father, You loved me so much that You gave Your own Son for me. Impress this loving-kindness on my heart that I may be always thankful for all You have given me. Help me to use my gifts in serving others. Amen.
(From Dear Father in Heaven, © 1963, 1977 Concordia Publishing House)

Day 1 2 3 4 5 6 7 8 9 10 11 12 13 14

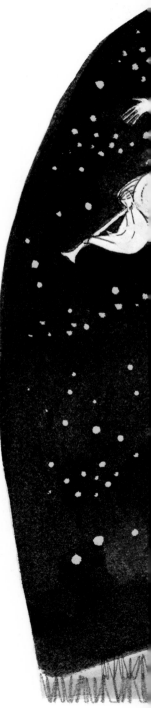

He hath sent Me to bind up the brokenhearted.
Isaiah 61:1, Revised Standard Version

The kings from the east were coming from their far countries to see the newborn King.

The angels sang the glad news to the shepherds watching their sheep near Bethlehem. "Behold," the angel of the Lord said, "I bring you good news of a great joy which will come to all the people; for to you is born this day in the city of David, a Savior, who is Christ the Lord."

Suddenly the sky was filled with other angels praising God, saying: "glory to God in the highest and on earth peace among men with whom He is pleased."

The long, long wait was over! In a little while, the world would know that the Messiah had come!

Activity:

Sing Christmas carols with your family. Listen to the words very carefully. Remember the promise God gave Eve, Abraham, Isaac, Jacob, Judah, Jesse, David and all the prophets. Sing as they would have sung-- "Joy to the World the Lord Has Come!"

Prayer:

On this day of Your birth, dear Lord, I again rejoice over the wonderful news that my Savior, my King, was born. How great is your love! Thank You for becoming a child on earth to fulfill the law for me and for taking away my sins. Because of Your love for me, fill me with love for others. Make me willing to share the Christmas joy, as well as all my other blessings, with those who need Your love. In your name I pray. Amen.

(From Dear Father in Heaven, © 1963, 1977 Concordia Publishing House)